Animals of Africa
GIRAFFES

by Tammy Gagne

FOCUS READERS

www.focusreaders.com

Focus Readers is distributed by North Star Editions:
sales@northstareditions.com | 888-417-0195

Produced for Focus Readers by Red Line Editorial.

Photographs ©: Delbars/Shutterstock Images, cover, 1; 1001slide/iStockphoto, 4–5, 24 (top right), 29; Red Line Editorial, 6; s2Bee/iStockphoto, 8; kimrawicz/iStockphoto, 10–11; WLDavies/iStockphoto, 12; Goddard_Photography/iStockphoto, 14–15; EcoPic/iStockphoto, 16–17; GlobalP/iStockphoto, 18; guenterguni/iStockphoto, 20; Janugio/iStockphoto, 22–23, 24 (top left); MorneGreen/iStockphoto, 24 (bottom right); Byrdyak/iStockphoto, 24 (bottom left); GomezDavid/iStockphoto, 26

ISBN
978-1-63517-263-8 (hardcover)
978-1-63517-328-4 (paperback)
978-1-63517-458-8 (ebook pdf)
978-1-63517-393-2 (hosted ebook)

Library of Congress Control Number: 2017935116

Printed in the United States of America
Mankato, MN
June, 2017

About the Author

Tammy Gagne has written more than 150 books for adults and children. She resides in northern New England with her husband and son. One of her favorite pastimes is visiting schools to talk to kids about the writing process.

TABLE OF CONTENTS

CHAPTER 1

Gentle Giants 5

CHAPTER 2

Above the Rest 11

THAT'S AMAZING!

Long Necks 14

CHAPTER 3

Tall and Fast 17

CHAPTER 4

Standing Up 23

Focus on Giraffes • 28
Glossary • 30
To Learn More • 31
Index • 32

GENTLE GIANTS

A giraffe stands alone. It watches as the others sleep. A few giraffes lie on the ground. There are few trees on the **savanna**. But some giraffes rest in their shade. The others rest standing up.

A giraffe looks out at the savanna.

Africa

Indian
Ocean

where giraffes live

Atlantic
Ocean

Wild giraffes live only in Africa.

Giraffes live in Africa. They spend

their time on the savanna. This is a

dry region. There are few trees or bushes. Giraffes are very tall. Their height lets them see long distances on the open landscape. They can spot **predators** easily.

A giraffe's home area can be as large as 50 square miles (130 sq. km). But they do not have **territories**.

FUN FACT

Giraffes are the tallest animals in the world.

 Giraffes are usually friendly to one another.

Giraffes are **social** animals. They live in groups. Sometimes one group of giraffes meets up with another. When this happens, the groups get along.

Male giraffes sometimes get into fights. They swing their necks. They may hit each other with their **ossicones**. But they usually do not hurt one another. A fight ends when one of the giraffes gives up.

CHAPTER 2

ABOVE THE REST

Giraffes have long legs. Their necks are long, too. This makes giraffes very tall. Their heads tower high above all other animals. Giraffes have ossicones on their heads. These are small horns.

A giraffe's ossicones are covered with hair.

Giraffes from the same area have similar coats.

Giraffes have spotted coats. The spots are brown. Light-colored hair surrounds the spots. Each animal has a different pattern.

Male giraffes are approximately 18 feet (5.5 m) tall. They can weigh up to 3,000 pounds (1361 kg). One giraffe's neck alone can weigh

600 pounds (272 kg). Females are smaller. They are approximately 14 feet (4.3 m) tall. They can weigh as much as 2,000 pounds (907 kg).

A giraffe has a large tongue. It is pink at the base. The tip of the tongue is a dark color. The tongue can be 21 inches (53 cm) long.

FUN FACT

A giraffe's heart is 2 feet (0.6 m) across. It has to be big to pump blood all the way up to the animal's brain.

LONG NECKS

A giraffe's neck sets it apart from other animals. This body part can be 6 feet (1.8 m) long. But even though the neck is incredibly long, it contains very few bones.

A giraffe has just seven bones in its entire neck. That is the same number of bones as a human neck. Like everything else about the giraffe, its neck bones are long. Each one can measure 10 inches (25 cm).

A giraffe's neck can be as long as its legs.

CHAPTER 3

TALL AND FAST

A giraffe has long legs. These help the animal move quickly. Giraffes can often outrun hyenas, leopards, and lions. Their legs are also powerful. A single kick can kill a predator such as a lion.

 Giraffes can run 35 miles per hour (56 km/h) in short bursts.

PARTS OF A GIRAFFE

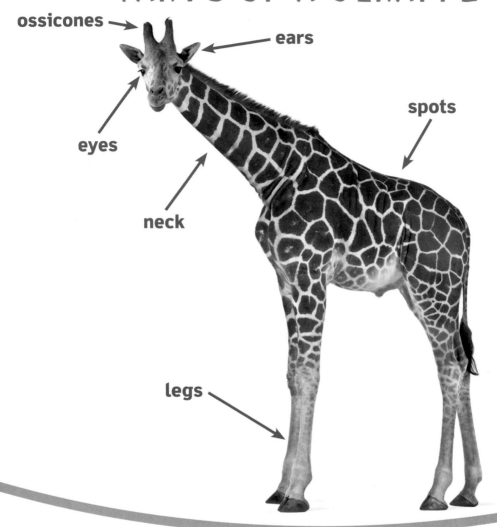

ossicones

ears

eyes

spots

neck

legs

Giraffes have excellent eyesight in daylight. Giraffes are usually silent during the day. They can

communicate using their eyes or touch. But they do not see as well at night. After the sun sets, they must use sounds. At night, giraffes communicate using humming noises. These sounds are low. Predators may not hear them. This helps keep giraffes safe.

FUN FACT

Birds sometimes perch on a giraffe's back. The birds eat bugs that live on the giraffe's coat.

 A giraffe bends over to take a drink of water.

These gigantic **mammals** sleep for only a half hour each day. Quick naps are enough to keep them going.

To drink water, giraffes must lower their necks and spread their legs wide apart. This stance makes it easier for predators to grab them. But giraffes do not place themselves in this position often. Giraffes need to drink only once every few days. Most of their water comes from the leaves they eat.

CHAPTER 4

STANDING UP

Female giraffes are called cows. A cow gives birth standing up. The baby is called a calf. When it is born, the calf falls approximately 5 feet (1.5 m) to the ground. The calf can run only 10 hours later.

A giraffe mother encourages her calf to stand up.

GIRAFFE LIFE CYCLE

Females usually have one calf at a time.

Calves can stand up 30 minutes after birth.

A tower can include 12 to 15 giraffes.

Calves become adults at three to six years.

24

Giraffes live in groups. These groups are called towers. A male giraffe is called a bull. Each tower is led by a bull.

Cows take turns watching the calves in their tower. If a mother leaves a calf alone, the calf will lie down. It waits for the mother to return.

FUN FACT

Most giraffes live for approximately 25 years.

 A giraffe eats acacia leaves.

Giraffes are herbivores. This means they eat only plants. They often eat leaves. Most of the leaves giraffes eat come from mimosa or acacia trees. They use their long tongues. A giraffe's tongue helps it grab leaves. It can grab leaves off even the tallest trees. The tongue helps it pick around sharp thorns, too. A single giraffe eats hundreds of pounds of leaves in one week.

FOCUS ON
GIRAFFES

Write your answers on a separate piece of paper.

1. Write a sentence that explains the main idea of Chapter 3.

2. Which part of the giraffe's appearance do you find most interesting? Why?

3. How often must giraffes drink?
    A. every few hours
    B. every few days
    C. every few weeks

4. Why might it be easier for a predator to grab a giraffe when drinking?
    A. Giraffes cannot run into the water.
    B. The giraffes' spotted coats are easier to see.
    C. The giraffes' stance brings them lower to the ground.

5. What does **coats** mean in this book?

Giraffes have spotted coats. The spots are brown. Light-colored hair surrounds the spots.

   A. hair that covers the body

   B. jackets

   C. patterns

6. What does **stance** mean in this book?

To drink water, giraffes must lower their necks and spread their legs wide apart. This stance makes it easier for predators to grab them.

   A. location

   B. distance

   C. body position

Answer key on page 32.

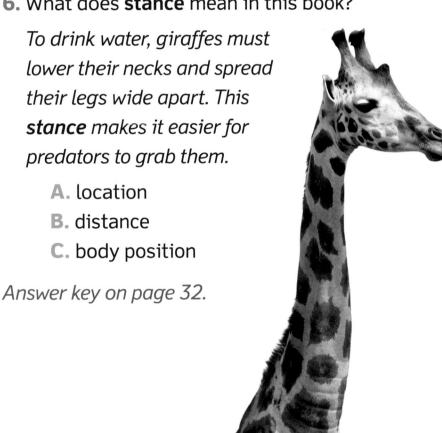

GLOSSARY

communicate
To make something known to others.

mammals
Animals that give birth to live babies, have fur or hair, and produce milk.

ossicones
The small horns on a giraffe's head.

predators
Animals that hunt other animals for food.

savanna
A grassland with few or no trees.

social
Likely to spend time with other animals of the same type.

territories
Areas that are defended by a group of animals.

TO LEARN MORE

BOOKS

Higgins, Melissa. *Grassland Ecosystems.* Minneapolis: Abdo Publishing, 2016.

Murray, Julie. *Giraffes*. Minneapolis: Abdo Publishing, 2012.

Spelman, Lucy. *National Geographic Animal Encyclopedia*. Washington, DC: National Geographic, 2012.

NOTE TO EDUCATORS

Visit **www.focusreaders.com** to find lesson plans, activities, links, and other resources related to this title.

INDEX

A
Africa, 6

C
calf, 23, 24, 25
communicate, 19

D
drink, 21

E
eyesight, 18-19

F
females, 13, 23, 24, 25
fights, 9
food, 27

H
height, 7, 12–13

L
legs, 11, 17

M
males, 9, 12, 25

N
necks, 11, 14

O
ossicones, 11

P
predators, 7, 17, 19, 21

S
savanna, 5, 6
sleep, 21
spots, 12

T
tongue, 13, 27
towers, 25

W
weight, 13

Answer Key: 1. Answers will vary; **2.** Answers will vary; **3.** B; **4.** C; **5.** A; **6.** C